Creating and Publishing Web Pages on the Internet

THE INTERNET LIBRARY

Creating and Publishing Web Pages on the Internet

Art Wolinsky

Enslow Publishers, Inc.

40 Industrial Road PO Box 38
Box 398 Aldershot
Berkeley Heights, NJ 07922 Hants GU12 6BP
USA UK

http://www.enslow.com

Library of Congress Cataloging-in-Publication Data

Wolinsky, Art.
      Creating and publishing Web pages on the Internet / Art Wolinsky.
      p. cm. — (The Internet library)
      Includes bibliographical references and index.
      Summary: A step-by-step explanation of how to design, create, and
maintain Web pages on the Internet. Includes addresses for some Web
sites created by students and places on the Internet that offer free Web
sites.
      ISBN 0-7660-1262-X
      1. Web sites—Design Juvenile literature. [1. Web sites. 2. World
Wide Web (Information retrieval system) 3. Internet (Computer
network)] I. Title. II. Series.
      TK5105.888.W644   1999
      005.7'2—dc21   99-23827
      005.75   CIP

Printed in the United States of America

10 9 8 7 6 5 4 3 2

To Our Readers:
All Internet addresses in this book were active and appropriate when we
went to press. Any comments or suggestions can be sent by e-mail to
Comments@enslow.com or to the address on the back cover.

Trademarks:
Most computer and software brand names have trademarks or registered
trademarks. The individual trademarks have not been listed here.

Cover Photo: © Index Stock Imagery

Contents

Introduction

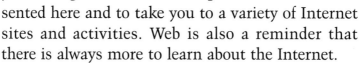

This is my friend Web. He will be appearing through-out the pages of this book to guide you through the information pre-sented here and to take you to a variety of Internet sites and activities. Web is also a reminder that there is always more to learn about the Internet.

We will show how you can put material on Web pages for others to see. You will learn how to create Web pages, but more important, you will learn how to create interesting Web pages that will appeal to others.

Almost anyone can make Web pages. First-time Web page authors often fall in love with the colors, the icons, the blinking words, and the animated pictures without really thinking about the message they are trying to get across. It is very easy to create pages that are nothing but "cotton candy for the eyes." The pages are pretty and flashy, but like cotton candy, they have no substance; when you bite into them, they melt away, leaving you hungry. Cotton candy is nice, but Web pages should be more than pretty. They should also be food for the mind.

You do not need an Internet connection to appreciate and learn from the information in this book. Because you are reading a book about creat-ing Web pages, I will assume you are comfortable using a Web browser. I will also assume you are familiar with using a word-processing program and can save and retrieve files from your computer.

Even though you do not need an Internet connection, you will need a computer, a word-processing program, a Web browser, and a graphics file (any file that ends in a .jpg or .gif extension) if you want to create the Web project in this book. There should be at least one file with a .jpg or .gif extension already on your computer. Use your file manager to find a file with a .jpg extension, and you can then choose and copy this file to use as an example in this book. If you do not have any of the required parts, you can still read this book and learn from it. After all, it is a good idea to read a driver's manual before trying to drive a car.

Quality over Flash:
When you are making your first Web page, keep it simple. Try not to add flashy graphics if you don't need to.

Chapter 1

Web Pages, Word Processing, and Tags

You may have wondered how Web pages are created. Well, you can create Web pages in several different ways, including through the use of a simple word-processing program. There are also HTML editors and Internet Web sites that will provide you with free Web space and easy-to-use templates and forms for creating your own Web pages.

I will discuss all these methods, but I will concentrate on giving you the basics of creating Web pages from scratch, using a simple computer word-processing program. It is important to learn the basics of HTML before using other methods of creating Web pages. Understanding the basics makes it easier for you to learn the other methods, because you will gain an understanding of what is happening behind the Web page display.

Normally, when you write something using a computer word-processing program, you can do text formatting by highlighting the text and then point-ing and clicking on icons or menu options. If you want to make a word bold, you just highlight it and then click on the icon for bold. If you want type ital-icized, you can highlight the text and then click on the proper icon or menu option.

If you could look behind the scenes of a word-processing program, you would see that before bold printing starts, there is an invisible marker, or tag, that tells the computer when to start printing bold type. There is also an invisible marker that tells the computer when to stop printing bold type.

This is not the case when you create Web pages by using a word-processing program. If you want a word to show up bold on a Web page, you must type in the information that tells the Web browser to show the word as bold. You do this by typing special tags before and after the words you want to be bold.

Take Your Time:
Making a Web page can get confusing. Go slowly, and make sure you learn the basics.

▶ Introduction to Tags

The tags you place on the page are called HTML tags. HTML stands for HyperText Markup Language, but it is not really a language, and it is not computer programming. Do not let the term confuse you; it is not difficult to learn. HTML is really simple.

Look at the following sentence as it appears on my word processor.

```
This sentence has four words in
bold, and four words in italics.
```

If we were to save the sentence as text and look at it with a Web browser, it would look like this.

```
This sentence has four words in
bold, and four words in italics.
```

All the formatting would be lost. The bolded and

the italicized words would become plain text when seen on the screen. The Web browser does not understand the same invisible tags that the word-processing program does. To make the words appear bold and italic, using the Web browser, you have to type in the special HTML tags as follows:

```
This sentence has <B>four words
in bold,</B> and <I>four words in
italics</I>.
```

When you save that in the word-processing program as text and then load it into the Web browser, it looks like this.

```
This sentence has four words in
bold, and four words in italics.
```

▶ Some Basic Tags and HTML Concepts

The concept of tags is easy to understand. On Web pages, if you want your text to have different looks, you must use one or more tags to make it so.

An HTML tag is always enclosed in a set of angle brackets. The angle brackets are created, using the < > symbols located on the comma and period keys of the keyboard. When a Web browser sees a letter, letters, word, or words inside a pair of these angle brackets, the browser looks at them as instructions to follow instead of displaying them.

In the example in the last section, there was one difference between the tag that turned on bold printing and the tag that turned it off—the forward slash. For example, <B> begins bold printing and </B> ends it.

It does not matter whether you use uppercase letters or lowercase letters to type tags. As far as the Web browser is concerned, when looking at tags, it sees them both the same way. All of the following tags work fine.

```
<B>These words would be bold.</B>
<b>These words would be bold.</b>
<B>These words would be bold.</b>
<b>These words would be bold.</B>
```

To add color to your text, the following tag is needed: <font color=*insert color*> So, for example, if you wanted your text to be red, you would type <font color=red>

There is one caution to keep in mind: You need tags even for spacing. The Web browser will ignore anything more than one space between words. It even ignores the end of a line or blank lines you create by hitting the Enter or Return key. Instead, there are tags to create extra spaces, tags to end lines, and tags to create blank lines. We will cover these tags when we actually create a Web page, later in the book.

Add Spacing:
You may have to add extra tags to keep the spacing between words that you want.

Chapter 2

Planning a Quality Web Site

Creating a Web site is easy. Creating a Web site that is well thought-out and holds the interest of visitors is not as easy. Even if you learn how to publicize your Web site so people come to visit, you want to make sure they do more than just visit the first page and then leave, never to return.

Probably the easiest and most popular first Web project is a personal Web page. It is very tempting to create a Web site that tells about you, your family, and your pets, but there are many reasons to avoid doing this. The most important reason to avoid this project is that it is never a good idea to post personal information about you or your family on the Internet. In addition, there are only a limited number of people who might be interested in you and your family. These people fall into two categories: your friends and your enemies.

You certainly do not want to create a Web site for people who might be up to no good and who want to gather information that might benefit themselves or harm you. And as far as your friends are concerned, they probably already know about you and what you would put on your page. Why go to all that trouble to tell them what they already know?

So what kind of Web site should you create? Any Web site that provides a unique service or information that is not easily found elsewhere is a good idea. Web sites based on research or schoolwork are great. They do not have to be huge sites with loads of pages. They can start out small and grow as quickly as you like.

▶ Pictures on Radio and Words on the TV

Before you begin to write the material that will appear on your Web site and create the tags, it is important to plan the Web pages you are going to create. Did you notice I said *Web pages*, not *Web page*? You could easily create a large Web site on a single page, but that would be poor Web site construction.

There are three major reasons for creating more than one page for your Web site. First, putting everything on one page could make a page that is ten to twelve screens long (or longer). Many people will see

---

Internet Addresses   Internet Facts   On Your Screen

Here are some Web sites created by students. Though they are not the first sites they created, they may give you ideas for your first project.

The Alphabet SuperHighway Exhibit Hall has programs created by students around the country:
< http://www.ash.udel.edu/ash/exhibit/exhibitframe.html >

The International Schools CyberFair draws class projects from around the globe:
< http://www.gsn.org/cf/index.html >

ThinkQuest is the Internet's premier contest and draws quality work from two-person and three-person teams from all over the world:
< http://www.thinkquest.org >

this and immediately decide there is too much to read. Studies show that most people will not read a single Web page that stretches over ten screens. They will, however, read the same material if it is spread over five screens, and are even more likely to read it if it is spread over more than five screens.

This leads to the second major reason for creating multiple Web pages. Part of the power of the Web is the ability to create pages that people—your visitors—can explore any way they want. The ability to create hyperlinks (words, icons, or other images that, when clicked on, jump to another place) makes Web pages easy to navigate. Putting NEXT and PREVIOUS buttons at the bottom of pages allows visitors who do not like to jump around to follow your pages in sequence. Creating a table of contents lets visitors explore your work another way. If you do not use all these techniques, you will not be using the Web to its greatest potential.

Imagine a radio show announcer saying, "Hey, gang, take a look at these pictures!" Pictures do not show up on the radio. Imagine tuning in to your favorite television show and, instead of actors and scenery, all you see is the script of the show scrolling slowly up the screen so you could read it. That would not make good use of the power of television. Putting a whole Web site on a single page is much like these examples. It does not take advantage of all the things you can do with the Web.

The final important reason for creating multiple Web pages is time. Large Web pages, especially those that contain many

More Than One Page:
The Internet makes it easy to jump from one Web page to another. Many people will create more than one page at a time.

pictures, can take a long time for a visitor to download to a computer. The slower the visitor's modem, the longer it will take for the page to load. Many Web pages are never even seen, because visitors get tired of waiting for the page to load and simply click off of the page and visit another site.

▶ Best Web Page Ideas Are All Around You

You never know when a Web site project may pop up.

- An eighty-two-year-old man came to school with a picture he took in Japan in 1945. Our students created a Web site and helped locate ten people in the fifty-year-old picture. The project ended with a videoconference that was broadcast on Japanese television.

  After seeing a news report of the project, I was contacted by a ninety-one-year-old community member. Some of my students interviewed him and turned his photo collection of the people of Okinawa, Japan, into a Web site.

- While waiting at the hospital for my mother-in-law to get X rays, I made arrangements for three of my students to create a Web site for the hospital.

Internet Addresses | Internet Facts | On Your Screen

Here are the addresses for the projects just listed:

<http://dune.srhs.k12.nj.us/www/etajima>

<http://dune.srhs.k12.nj.us/www/okinawa>

<http://dune.srhs.k12.nj.us/soch>

When a tall Web and a shorter Web stand back to back, their arms are still the same distance from the floor. This observation forms the basis for the pages we will learn to create in this book.

Another great Web project began at a Fourth of July picnic. It is the Web project I will use to teach you about HTML.

I was at a barbecue at my friend Buddy's house. Buddy is a golfer and is well over six feet tall. He told me he went to buy a set of golf clubs and asked the salesperson to show him a set of long clubs.

The salesperson asked him why he wanted long clubs. My friend looked at him sort of funny and said, "Because I'm tall." The salesperson just smiled and said, "That doesn't matter. Your arms are the same distance from the ground as shorter people's."

Reaching Your Goal:
Our first Web page will be simple to make. In the future, you will learn how to make Web pages that are more complicated.

That surprised my friend, and his story surprised me. To check it out, we stood side by side. He is about six feet four inches tall, and I am five feet eight inches tall, but when we stood side by side, our fingertips were almost the identical distance from the floor.

That gave me the idea for the Web site that I will teach you to create. I will take you step-by-step through the creation of a Web page that shows people how to do this simple, interesting science experiment. Once it is finished, you might even want to turn it into a class project.

Chapter 3

Starting Your Web Pages

You might think we are ready to start building Web pages, but we are not there yet. Before starting the Web site construction, you need to create a plan for your site. The plan may be an outline, a narrative, a storyboard, or some other form, but it should show how you want your site to look and to work. The plan does not have to be detailed, and it can change as you build the site.

Here is an example of what a simple plan might look like:

My Web site will have

- a title page that contains an introduction to the experiment;
- a table of contents;
- a procedure page;
- a results page;
- a conclusion page.

You will construct the first three of the five pages listed here. I will leave the last two for you to complete if you want to conduct the experiment and if you feel up to the challenge of completing the site on your own.

▶ Universal Tags

Now we are ready to begin creating the Web site. You will use your computer's word-processing

Creating a Storyboard

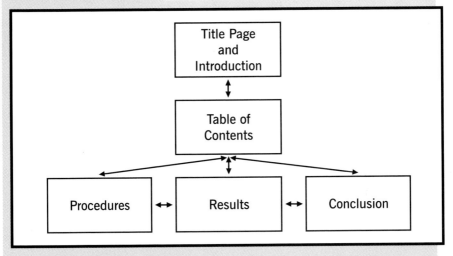

Here is what a storyboard that maps out the look of a Web page might look like.

program to create the pages. Any word-processing program will do, but the simpler, the better. Simple word-processing programs use little memory, and you are not going to need the features of a powerful one. All you will be doing is typing words and creating tags to format the text.

If you are using a computer with Microsoft Windows, you might find it easy to use one of the built-in word-processing programs such as Wordpad, Notepad, or Write. If you are using a Mac, you might use SimpleText, which comes with the Mac. As I said, any word-processing program will do. The one thing you *must* remember is to save your work as a text file. All word-processing programs allow you to do this, but it will add an extra step or two to your normal saving procedure. If you are not sure how to save things in text file format, consult the program's manual.

As you work, I will explain what I want you to do. I will often tell you to save a copy of what you have done so far as a text file. Any new typing I want you to add to the text will always be indicated in bold. Anything you have already typed will appear in normal print.

▶ Your First Tag

Open a new document in your word-processing program. Before we start creating the words we want our users to see, we must create some tags that all Web pages have in common. These tags will be read by the Web browser but not seen by your visitors. The first tag tells the Web browser that the page is an HTML document. This tag is actually a set of tags. The first tag on the page tells the Web browser where the page starts, and the last tag tells the browser where the page ends. In your document, type the following:

```
<HTML>
</HTML>
```

Bracket Boomerang:
It's very important to use angle brackets in your HTML code. Without the brackets, your Web page will not work.

Be sure to use the < and > symbols (angle brackets), not the (and) (parenthesis) or the [and] (brackets). Be sure to include the / (slash) in the end tag.

<HTML> marks the beginning of your page, and </HTML> is the last thing on your page. Two entire sections will fit in between the tags. The first section is the header, and the second is the body. Any tags you put in the header are not part of your Web page display. They are there to give instructions to the

browser. Any tags you place in the body section will cause things to appear so that your visitors can see them.

Now you will type in a pair of tags that define the header area. These tags will be placed in between the two you just typed.

```
<HTML>
<HEAD>
</HEAD>
</HTML>
```

Ending Brackets:
In HTML coding, angle brackets have to be in pairs—one to start the code, and one to end it.

It does not make much sense yet, does it? Don't worry. It will shortly.

Before going any further, you should save your document. It is always a good idea to save your work every few minutes. Doing so prevents you from losing your work if you have a power problem or if the computer freezes up. *You will also have to save before viewing what you have typed as a Web page.*

IMPORTANT: Be sure to save all your Web work in a single folder. If your Web site has many pages and many pictures, save them in the same folder. When you get to be an expert, you will learn how to save work in different folders, but for now, save your work in a single folder.

Do not forget, you must *save the document as a text file.* When you save the document, there are a few important rules to remember about naming it.

1. Never use punctuation or spaces in your file names.

2. Your file name must end in **.html** (Note: If

you are using Windows 3.1 or an earlier version, the file name must end in **.htm**).

3. Though not required, it is a good idea to use only lowercase letters in your file names.

When you save this document, you will name it **fingers.html**

NOTE: I purposely did not end the last sentence with a period, because some people would type it as part of the name, and that would confuse the computer. There will be other times when I will end sentences with .html. Do not think the period at the end of the sentence is part of the file name or the URL (universal resource locator, address). *Internet file names and URLs never end with a period.*

Now that you have saved the document, you are almost ready to take a look at it with the Web browser, but first you must add one more tag in the header area. There are many things you can include in the header area, but for this page, you will only put in one thing. That is the title tag. We will type the beginning tag <TITLE>, followed by the title we choose for our page, and then the ending tag </TITLE>.

Most HTML formatting is done with pairs of codes enclosed in brackets. If you forget one of these codes, the formatting may not work.

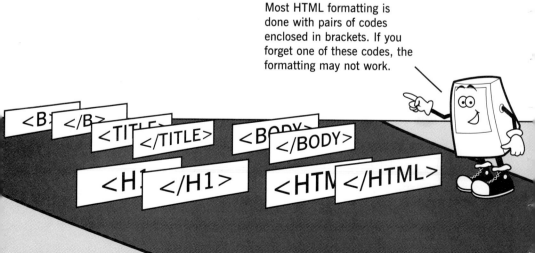

Do not confuse the title tag with the file name you just used when you saved the page. They are used for different purposes. You will see the difference in a few minutes.

Type in the following new information.

```
<HTML>
<HEAD>
<TITLE>A Science Experiment at
Arm's Length</TITLE>
</HEAD>
</HTML>
```

You are almost ready to look at the results of your work, but first, you must save your work again. Because you have saved it once and it has a name, all you have to do is go to the *File* menu of the word-processing program and then click on *Save*. Do not close your word-processing program, though.

The next step is to open your Web browser, if it is not already open. You are probably using Netscape Navigator or Microsoft Internet Explorer. Once you open your browser, you must click on its *File* menu and then select the option that will allow you to open the Web page you have been creating with your word-processing program.

In Netscape Navigator, you must click on the *File* menu and then *Open File*. From there, you will click on the *Choose File* button, and then go to the file you have just saved (**fingers.html**) and open it.

Viewing Your Work:
It's fun to view your Web page in different stages. But do not forget to save your work often so that you do not lose anything.

Inserting a Title

If you have done everything correctly, this is what you will see in your browser depending on whether you used Microsoft Internet Explorer (top) or Netscape (bottom).

In Microsoft Internet Explorer, you must click on *Open*. From there, you will click on the *Browse* button, and then go to the file you have just saved (**fingers.html**) and open it.

If you are looking at your Web browser instead of the title bars above, at first glance you might think there is nothing on your page. Technically you are right, but look at the bar on the very top of each browser's window. You will see the words *A Science Experiment at Arm's Length*. These are the words you placed before the beginning and ending title tags.

You should now see the difference between the file name (fingers.html) and the title (A Science Experiment at Arm's Length) that is inside the title tags.

Now, using your word-processing program again, you can create the body tags and put text on the page. The starting body tag <BODY> is placed right after the title, and the ending body tag </BODY> is placed just before the ending </HTML> tag.

```
<HTML>
<HEAD>
<TITLE>A Science Experiment at Arm's
Length</TITLE>
</HEAD>
```
<BODY>

</BODY>
```
</HTML>
```

The rest of the material for the first page will be typed between the two body tags.

Except for the words between the title tags, each of your Web pages should start out looking like the above example. Each page should have a good descriptive title between the title tags for two reasons. First, it is helpful to those who visit your site, and more important, search engines use the title to index Web pages.

Title Your Page:
If you use a descriptive title for your Web page, you will help people understand your page better.

▶ Take a Break

Now is a good time to take a break. It is not that I think you are overworked; I just want you to know what you have to do to get started again after you take a break. I also want you to know how to get restarted if you have a problem and do not know what to do. *You may want to place a piece of paper at this page in your book so you can get back here easily.*

Close the word-processing program and the Web browser.

To restart:

1. In the word-processing program, find the file you were working with (in this case, **fingers.html**) and open it.

2. Open your Web browser.

   a) Go to the *File* menu, and depending on whether you are using Netscape Navigator or Microsoft Internet Explorer, select the appropriate option, *Open File* or *Open*.

   b) From there, depending on whether you are using Netscape Navigator or Microsoft Internet Explorer, select either *Choose File* or *Browse*.

   c) Find the file you want to work with (in this case, **fingers.html**) and open it.

You should now be ready to continue working on your Web page.

Chapter 4

A Peek at Your First Page

I want you to see what your first page will look like when it is finished. It will help you understand the tags I will cover and allow me to move faster and cover more territory with you.

You will learn six new tags in order to complete this page. The first tag you will learn is the tag to create the lines that go across the screen above and below the headline. The next tags will be the tags that create the headline and center it on the page.

You will create a tag for the picture. From there, you will type in the text and learn about paragraph tags.

Paragraphs are not indented. Instead, they are separated by blank lines. The reason for this is simple. If you remember, I told you that anything more than a single space requires a special tag. To get the five spaces you would normally use to indent a paragraph, you would have to type one space and then the tag for a space four times. You would have to type this:

```
    
```

That would be a real pain. Instead of doing all that typing, you will use a simple tag that ends the paragraph and inserts a blank line.

Finally, you will learn how to create a hyperlink

The Finished Product

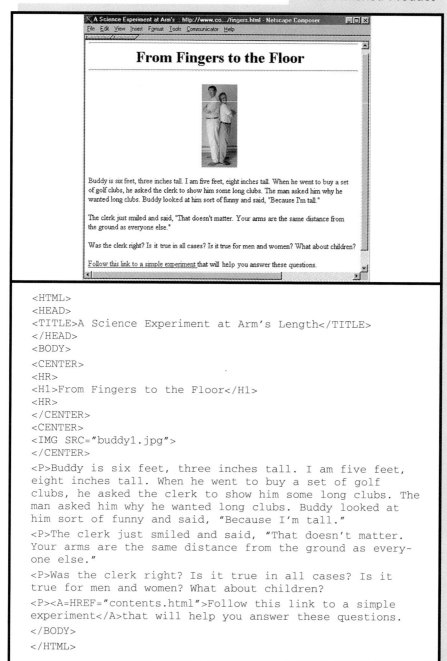

```
<HTML>
<HEAD>
<TITLE>A Science Experiment at Arm's Length</TITLE>
</HEAD>
<BODY>

<CENTER>
<HR>
<H1>From Fingers to the Floor</H1>
<HR>
</CENTER>
<CENTER>
<IMG SRC="buddy1.jpg">
</CENTER>

<P>Buddy is six feet, three inches tall. I am five feet,
eight inches tall. When he went to buy a set of golf
clubs, he asked the clerk to show him some long clubs. The
man asked him why he wanted long clubs. Buddy looked at
him sort of funny and said, "Because I'm tall."

<P>The clerk just smiled and said, "That doesn't matter.
Your arms are the same distance from the ground as every-
one else."

<P>Was the clerk right? Is it true in all cases? Is it
true for men and women? What about children?

<P><A=HREF="contents.html">Follow this link to a simple
experiment</A>that will help you answer these questions.

</BODY>
</HTML>
```

When we are finished, our first Web page will look like this.
The coding used to create the page is shown below it.

to take the user to the next page. Your hyperlink will be underlined and blue before you click on it and purple after you click on it. When you become a skilled Web master, you will be able to change the colors, but we will not get that far in this book.

When you click on a hyperlink, something happens. It could take you to another page in the site or to a page somewhere else on the Web. It could link to a picture, play a sound file, show a movie, or do any number of other possible actions. On your page, it will link to another page on your Web site.

By the time you are finished with the first page, you will have most of the skills you need to begin creating Web pages. Of course, there are many tags and techniques I cannot cover in this book, but later, Web will point you to places on the Internet where you can find all of the advanced techniques.

▶ Type, Save, and Reload Technique

You are now ready to add more tags to what you already have. We will use a technique I call TSR. It stands for *Type, Save,* and *Reload.* You will Type with the word-processing program and then Save your changes. Then you will go to your Web browser and click on the *Reload* or *Refresh* button to see the changes you had made when you typed. Then, you will TSR over and over until the page is done.

Remember, if you get in trouble, you can always go back to the "Take a Break" section I asked you to mark. It will get you started again.

Chapter 5

Creating the First Page

There are six different sizes for headlines. The tags begin with the letter *H* and a number. The largest headline is <H1> and the smallest is <H6>. Let's try the TSR technique and place the headline on your page. If you do not have fingers.htm loaded in the Web browser, do it now. (You will create the lines and center the headline later.) In the word processor, type the new material you see printed in bold in the following text:

```
<HTML>
<HEAD>
<TITLE> A Science Experiment at
Arm's Length </TITLE>
</HEAD>
<BODY>
<H1> From Fingers to the Floor </H1>
</BODY>
</HTML>
```

Save your changes.

Go to your Web browser and click on the *Reload* button. You should now see something similar to the example on page 31.

Take a few minutes to experiment with the headlines. Use the TSR technique and change the headline size, using the other numbers. You will find that most of your headlines will be sizes 1, 2, or 3. Make sure your starting and ending numbers

Adding a Headline

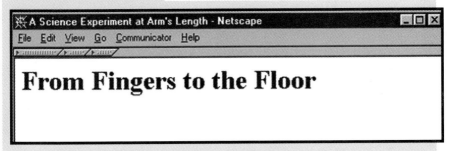

If everything was done correctly, your headline should look like this.

in the tags are the same. You cannot start with size 1 and end with a different number.

A common mistake people make when inserting tags is forgetting to use the slash in the ending tag. For example, you might see the following:

```
<H2>My Web Page<H2>
```

When the TSR technique is used, it may look fine, but when you continue making the page, everything from that point on will STILL be in size 2 headlines, because the Web browser saw the opening <H2> tag and will continue making headlines until it sees the closing </H2> tag.

If you do something and it does not turn out the way you think it should have, the first thing to do is check to see whether you have correct starting and ending tags.

▶ Centering Text

By now you should be getting the idea that tags are not difficult. The tags often use words or letters that represent what the tag does. One tag turns on a feature and the second turns it off.

Are you ready for a challenge? Do you think you can figure out how to center the headline on the page so that it looks like the example on page 33? If you are ready for the challenge, use the TSR technique and give it a try. If you have problems, check the section in this chapter where I showed you how to center the text.

How did you do? Check the text below to make sure you did everything correctly.

```
<HTML>
<HEAD>
<TITLE>A Science Experiment at
Arm's Length </TITLE>
</HEAD>
<BODY>
<CENTER>
<H1>From Fingers to the Floor</H1>
</CENTER>
</BODY>
</HTML>
```

Because you were centering the headline, you should have put the starting <CENTER> tag before the <H1> and put the ending </CENTER> tag after the </H1>.

By the way, putting tags on lines by themselves is not required. The browser reads from left to right and from top to bottom. As long as the tags are in the correct order, they will work. I separate tags because they are easier to read that way. If I have to go back to check a mistake, it is easier to find when the tags are separated.

I choose to write the tags this way.

```
<CENTER>
<H1>From Fingers to the Floor</H1>
</CENTER>
```

The same tags could have been written this way.

```
<CENTER><H1> From Fingers to the
Floor </H1></CENTER>
```

In fact, the entire page could have been written as one long continuous line, but a mistake would be very difficult to find.

▶ Horizontal Rules

The lines that are drawn above and below the headline are called horizontal rules (<HR>), and they work a little differently from the way the tags you have seen so far do. All the tags so far start with an opening tag that is followed by some words that are acted on by the tag, and then end with a closing tag. When you are drawing a line from one side of the

Centering the Headline

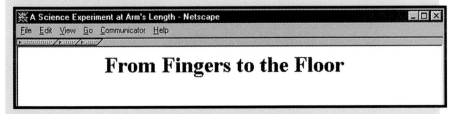

Centering the headline should look like this.

screen to another, there are no words that fall between the starting and ending tags. It would be silly to have to type <HR></HR>. For this reason, the creators of HTML decided that all you would need for this is a single tag, <HR>.

Because we want one line above the headline and one below, we have to put the <HR> tag in two places. Ready for another challenge? Use the TSR technique and see whether you can get the page to look like the example below. Check your work in the coding following the picture.

Adding Rules

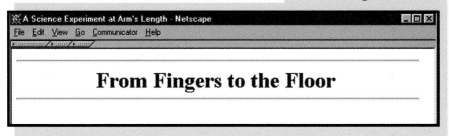

The lines above and below the headline are the latest additions to the page.

```
<HTML>
<HEAD>
<TITLE> A Science Experiment at
Arm's Length </TITLE>
</HEAD>
<BODY>
<HR>
<CENTER>
<H1> From Fingers to the Floor
</H1>
</CENTER>
<HR>
</BODY>
</HTML>
```

You could have placed the <HR> tags after the <CENTER> and before the </CENTER>. As you experiment, you will find there is often more than one correct way to do things.

▶ A Word About Pictures

You are about to add a picture. Any picture will do for practice, and you may have several pictures on your computer that you can use. (Feel free to use any file on your computer that has a .jpg or .gif ending.)

If you do not have access to a picture, it is not a big problem. You will just see an icon on your page where the picture would appear if you had one.

In the computer world, dozens of different programs create pictures, or graphics. Graphics have three-letter endings, called extensions. For Web pages, only two types of pictures can be used. They are .jpg and .gif pictures.

▶ Getting the Picture

To copy a picture if you are connected to the Internet, you can go to any Web site. The following picture and coding are my example. (Your picture may be different.)

Here is what you have to do to copy a picture to your computer from a Web page. It is slightly different for Macintosh and Windows systems. Please follow the correct instructions.

Windows

Point to the picture you want to copy with your mouse.

Grab a Picture:
It's easy to take a picture off a Web page to use in your practice page.

Click on the picture with the RIGHT mouse button and a menu will appear.

Click with the LEFT mouse button on the Save Image As... option and the *Save As* box will appear.

Save the picture in the same folder as fingers.html and do not change the name that is already there.

Macintosh
Point to the picture with your mouse.

Hold the mouse button down for a few seconds; a menu will appear.

Slide over to *Save Image As...* option and click on it. The *Save As* box will appear.

Save the picture in the same folder as fingers.html and do not change the name that is already there.

That is all there is to it. You can copy almost any picture from any Web page that way.

▶ Finding a .JPG File on Your Computer

Search your C drive for a file that ends in a .JPG extension. Choose one file, then follow the directions given earlier in the "Getting the Picture" section.

IMPORTANT: If you just traveled to another Web page to get a picture, you are no longer looking at the page you are creating. If you use the TSR technique now, you will have problems, because the *Reload* button just reloads the page you are viewing.

Instead, click the *Back* button on the browser and move back to the page you are creating. Then, when you hit *Reload*, things will work properly. If you are still having problems, follow the steps in the "Take a Break" section.

▶ Putting the Picture on Your Page

We are now ready to put the picture on your Web page. This tag is a little different from the others. It looks like this:

```
<IMG SRC="buddy1.jpg">
```

IMG SRC stands for image source. The name of the picture file must be enclosed in the quotation marks. Notice, there is a space between IMG and SRC, but no other spaces.

Now we have a slightly more difficult challenge. We also want the picture to be centered. You will have to add a set of center tags. Do you think you are ready to do two things, using the TSR technique? Can you place the picture on the page *and* center it? Try. If all goes well, your page will look like the work in the text that follows.

New Coding:
With a few words of coding, it's also easy to add a picture to your Web page.

```
<HTML>
<HEAD>
<TITLE> A Science Experiment at
Arm's Length </TITLE>
</HEAD>
<BODY>
<HR>
<CENTER>
<H1> From Fingers to the Floor </H1>
</CENTER>
```

```
<HR>
<CENTER>
<IMG SRC="buddy1.jpg">
</CENTER>
</BODY>
</HTML>
```

▶ Paragraphs

The paragraph tag looks like this <P> and is treated the same as the <HR> tag: The closing </P> is not required. You could put <P> at the beginning of a paragraph and a </P> at the end, but because the end of one paragraph also marks the start of a new one, the HTML programmers felt only the <P> tag was necessary. On your Web page, you will see that a blank line now separates the text, indicating a new paragraph.

It is now time to type in the four paragraphs that will almost complete the first page of the Web site. The only thing you will then need to complete the page will be the link to the next page in your Web site. Because the text box is getting rather long and because you have seen the tags many times, I will leave out most of what we have already typed in order to save space for more important things.

```
<CENTER>
<IMG SRC="buddy1.jpg"
</CENTER>
<P>Buddy is six feet three inches
tall. I am five feet eight inches
tall. When he went to buy a set of
golf clubs, he asked the clerk to
show him some long clubs. The man
```

```
asked him why he wanted long clubs.
Buddy looked at him sort of funny
and said, "Because I'm tall."
<P>The clerk just smiled and said,
"That doesn't matter. Your arms are
the same distance from the ground
as shorter people's."
<P>Was the clerk right? Is it true
in all cases? Is it true for men
and women? What about children?
<P>Follow this link to a simple
experiment that will answer these
questions.
</BODY>
</HTML>
```

▶ Creating Hyperlinks

Hyperlinks are the true power of Web pages. They allow you to create pages that can take your visitors to millions of other Web pages, allow them to listen to sounds, view movies, or do many other exciting things. Hyperlinks are probably the most powerful thing you will learn at this point. Creating them is also a little more complicated than creating the other tags you have made.

The hyperlink tag is called an anchor tag, and it has a number of parts. The best way to explain it is to show you how we will make our tag, and then show you examples of other uses of anchor tags.

The last paragraph you typed looked like this:

```
<P>Follow  this  link  to  a  simple
experiment that will answer these
questions.
```

You want the words *Follow this link to a simple experiment* to become a blue, underlined link that will take the person to the next page, which is a simple table of contents. Use the TSR technique to make the following changes to what you have already typed. When you reload the page you should see the link, but do not test it yet. (We have not yet made the second page, so the link cannot go anywhere.)

```
<P> <A HREF="contents.html"> Follow
this link to a simple experiment </A>
that will answer these questions.
```

The <A starts the anchor. The HREF stands for Hyper Reference. Be careful not to reverse the letters when you type this tag. This completes the first page of your Web site. You can now pat yourself on the back for a job well done.

▶ More About Anchor Tags

Before we go to page two, I want to talk more about the powerful anchor tags. What goes in between the quotation marks depends on what you want to happen when visitors click on the link. In this case, you want them to go to the page you will name contents.html. That page must be saved in the same folder as the fingers.html Web page.

If you wanted to display a picture, play a sound, or play a movie that is saved in the same folder as the Web page, you would place the full name of the sound or movie file in quotes.

If you wanted to send the user to a different Web site or somewhere other than the current folder, you would have to put the entire Internet URL between the quotes.

Here are some examples of other uses for anchor tags. (You can use any .wav or .gif file to create your own examples.)

- Here is my little sister singing <A HREF="song.wav"> Happy Birthday.</A>

  The words *Happy Birthday*, would be the link (blue and underlined). Clicking on them would play the sound file named song.wav, as long as it was saved in the same folder with the Web page.

- Here is a really neat <A HREF= "http://www.coolbirthday.com"> birthday site. </A>

  Here the words *birthday site* would be the link that takes the visitor to a different Web site. (Note: www.cool-birthday.com is not a real site.) Because it is not in the same folder as the current Web page, I had to include the full URL.

- Here is a picture of <A HREF="cake.gif"> my sister's birthday cake.</A>

  This would display a picture named cake.gif on a page by itself, when the person clicked on the words *my sister's birthday cake*. Note that this is different from <IMG SRC="cake.gif">, which would display the picture on the current page without any clicking.

Do you understand all that? I hope so, because the next example gets a little tricky, but it is powerful and fun.

Internet Music:
You can also add music and video files to your web page for other people to hear and see.

Suppose you wanted to have a picture of your sister's cake on the page, and when the user clicked on it, he or she could hear your sister sing "Happy Birthday." Here is how to turn a picture named cake.gif, into a hyperlink that plays the sound file named song.wav.

• Click on the cake to hear my sister sing "Happy Birthday."

```
<A HREF="song.wav"><IMG SRC=
"cake.gif"> </A>
```

Chapter 6

On to Page Two

I have two more pages and a few more tags to show you. When that is done, you will be able to add more pages to complete the site in any way you choose. I will use a new technique to help you through this last section.

The way I learned to create Web pages was through a combination of tutorials, such as the one you are going through now, and by looking at tags and pages that were created by people who made Web sites I liked. It would be great if you saw a Web page that you liked on the Internet and were able to look behind the scenes to see what the author had written to create the page. Well, you can do that.

In this section, I will

- take you though the steps that allow you to see the next two pages with your browser;
- show you how to look behind the scenes at the tags I used to create them;
- explain how to save a page directly from the Internet to your computer;
- explain how to open the saved page and change it.

I will also be providing pictures of the pages and copies of the tags on the pages. After that, you can examine the pages to see how to use the tags you learned for the first page, and then learn the final tags that will be covered in this book.

You should by now be comfortable with the TSR method and can use it as you choose.

▶ A Look at the Last Two Pages

The examples on page 45 show what all three pages—the first and the last two—will look like.

Looking at the example on page 46, the first thing you may notice is a new picture on the page. I have called this picture **buddy1.jpg** and have saved it in my folder along with my **fingers.html** file. Your picture can be any file that ends in a .jpg or .gif extension. If you do not have one of these files, and do not have an Internet connection, you will instead see an icon in place of the picture when you make the page.

▶ Examine the HTML for the Contents

Take Another Look:
When you are making your Web page, it's a good idea to check your progress from time to time.

Now that you have seen what the page looks like, let us take a look at the HTML that was used to create it. Here is the coding for the file I have called **contents.html** used to create the Web page shown on page 46.

```
<HTML>
<HEAD>
<TITLE>Table of Contents</TITLE>
</HEAD>
<BODY>
<HR>
<!--Let us turn on centering
for a whole section-->
```

Multiple Page Preview

From Fingers to the Floor

Buddy is six feet, three inches tall. I am five feet, eight inches tall. When he went to buy a set of golf clubs, he asked the clerk to show him some long clubs. The man asked him why he wanted long clubs. Buddy looked at him sort of funny and said, "Because I'm tall."

The clerk just smiled and said, "That doesn't matter. Your arms are the same distance from the ground as everyone else."

Was the clerk right? Is it true in all cases? Is it true for men and women? What about children?

Follow this link to a simple experiment that will help you answer these questions.

Conducting the Experiment

Procedure
Results
Conclusion

[BACK]

Fingertips Experiment

Materials:

- Meter stick to measure distance from floor to fingertips
- Height chart or tool to measure a person's height
- Pencil or pen
- Paper

Procedure:

1. Record the person's age.
2. Record the person's sex.
3. Measure and record the person's height.
4. Measure and record the distance from the floor to the person's fingertips.
5. Repeat the procedure with as many subjects as you can.
6. Compile the data and analyze it.
7. Write your conclusions.

[BACK]

Here is a sneak preview of what three pages of our Web site will look like.

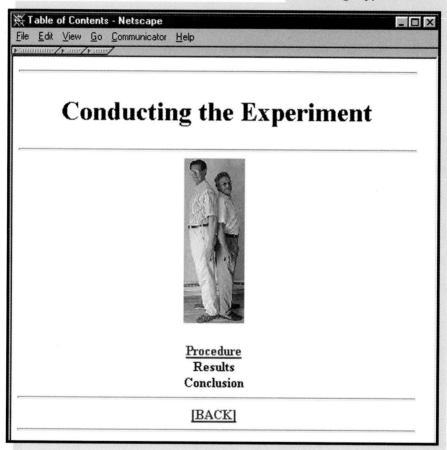

Notice the use of hyperlinks to guide users through the contents page of our Web site.

```
<CENTER>
<H1>Conducting the Experiment</H1>
<HR>
<P>
<IMG SRC="buddy2.jpg">
<P>
<!--Let us turn on bold for a
section-->
<B>
<P>
<A HREF="experiment.html">[Proce-
dure]</A> <BR>
Results <BR>
Conclusion <BR>
<HR>
<A HREF="fingers.html">[BACK]</A>
<HR>
<!--Let us turn off centering and
bold for the whole section-->
</B>
</CENTER>
</BODY>
</HTML>
```

We will examine the HTML code one section at a time to review what you have already learned, and then pick up a few new tags and tricks.

As we look at the coding on pages 44 and 47, we see the familiar starting <HTML> tag, the header tags with the title tags, the beginning body tag, and the horizontal rule tag. But the next tag is new. This tag is a very special and useful one that does nothing at all.

You may wonder why a tag that does nothing at all can be useful. Well, this tag can be used to input information that is ignored entirely by the browser and is not seen by visitors to the Web site. By using this tag, you can write reminders to yourself or write notes to other people who might be working on your Web page with you. Here is the way to construct the tag.

```
<!--Use any words you want-->
```

In this case, I used it to tell you about a short-cut I was using with the <CENTER> tag. Because everything on this page is centered, you do not have to use tags for each line. You can just turn on centering at the top of the page and then turn it off at the bottom.

The next section of HTML looks like this.

```
<H1>Conducting the Experiment</H1>
<HR>
<P>
<IMG SRC="buddy2.jpg">
<P>
```

Crack the Code:
HTML codes can be difficult to read at first. But if you take your time, you should be able to read through it.

You should be familiar with the head-line, horizontal rule, paragraph, and image source tags, but you may not understand the use of the <P> paragraph tags, because there are no words there, just a picture.

These tags are used to create a blank line above and below the picture. Putting the blank line above the picture is just for spacing. It looks better that way. Putting the blank line below the picture is impor-tant, because without it, the words that follow would be next to the picture instead of below it.

Next you see:

```
<!--Let us turn on bold for a
section-->
<B>
<P>
<A HREF="experiment.html">
Procedure</A> <BR>
Results <BR>
Conclusion <BR>
```

It starts with a note telling you we are turning on bold printing for the section. Because everything else on the page is going to be bold, we can just turn on bold here and turn off bold at the bottom of the page.

The next line uses the anchor tag to create a link to the page that gives the details of the experiment. When a person clicks on the word *Procedure*, they will be taken to the page saved as *experiment.html*.

At the end of that line is the new tag, <BR>. This tag is a line-break, and it is used much like the <P> tag, with one small difference. The <P> tag inserts a blank line and then starts a new line. The <BR> tag breaks the line where you type the tag and then starts a new line without putting in a blank line. Using <P> or <BR> is usually just a matter of deciding how you want your page to look. You can experiment and decide what you like best.

You may be wondering why I have included the next two lines. The Procedure page is the last page you will create

Reminders:
You can use certain HTML codes to leave reminders for yourself in the coding.

as part of this project, but the Results page and the Conclusion page are documents you may want to create on your own. You can turn them into links later. If you do not plan to create these pages, you can just delete those two lines.

End the page with:

Add a Link:
Linking between your Web pages will help people browse easily through your Web site.

```
<HR>
<A> HREF="fingers.html">[BACK]</A>
<HR>
<!—Let us turn off centering
and bold for the whole
section—>
</B>
</CENTER>
</BODY>
</HTML>
```

This last section is important. It is called the navigation bar. It is always a good idea to place links on a page that allow the user to move around the site. Sometimes the navigation bar is on the bottom of the page, and at other times it is on the top or the left side. Putting it on the side requires the use of an advanced device called frames.

Your navigation bar is made with a pair of horizontal rules and an anchor tag between them. The anchor tag makes a link out of the word *BACK*. This allows the user to go back to the first page of the Web site. You probably know that visitors could go back simply by clicking the *BACK* button on their browser, but you would be amazed by how many new users do not know about the *BACK* button.

In this case, you just offer one place to go, but as you build more Web sites, you might see other links such as

[PREVIOUS]   [HOME]   [NEXT]

You see a note about turning off centering and bold type, followed by the ending </BODY> and </HTML> tags. This brings us to the last page, where you will learn two new tags.

▶ Looking Behind the Scenes of a Web Page

Now that you have learned how to write the HTML coding for this page yourself, I'll let you in on a little secret. If you have an Internet connection, you would not have had to type anything at all to save this page. You can copy and save the HTML coding from any Web page directly from the Internet. The two pages you have created so far, and the third page to follow can all be found and saved from the following Web site:

Title page
http://www.concentric.net/~awolinsk/
experiment/fingers.html

Contents page
http://www.concentric.net/~awolinsk/
experiment/contents.html

Procedures page
http://www.concentric.net/~awolinsk/
experiment/experiment.html

The .jpg pictures of the author and Buddy can be found at:

> **buddy1.jpg** can be found on the fingers.html page
>
> **buddy2.jpg** can be found on the contents.html page
>
> **buddy3.jpg** which you haven't seen yet can be found on this page:

Experiment in Progress
http://www.concentric.net/~awolinsk/
experiment

Type in the address and you will see the page as it appears in this book.

Looking at the HTML coding behind any Web page

To see the coding that makes up these Web pages or any other Web page, using Netscape, click on the *View* menu, then click on *Page Source*. In Internet Explorer, click the *View* menu, then click on *Source*.

To copy the HTML code from any Web page

Just go to the File menu of your Web browser and click on *Save As* or *Save As File*, depending on whether you have Netscape Navigator or Microsoft Explorer. When the *Save* box comes up, be sure you are saving the page in the same folder as the other page and pictures, and be sure you are saving it as an HTML file. The file will be saved as the same file name unless you name it differently.

To copy any Picture File (.jpg or .gif file) from the Internet

If you are using Windows, place your mouse cursor over the photo, then click on the right mouse button. Then click on *Save Image As* and save it into the same folder as your other work. If you are using a Macintosh, point to the picture with your mouse, and hold the mouse button down for a few seconds until a menu appears. Slide over to *Save Image As...* option and click on it. The *Save As* box will appear. The file will be saved as the same file name unless you name it differently.

▶ The Author's Web Page and E-Mail

You can see what the author is up to these days by going to his Web page at:

http://www.concentric.net/~awolinsk

and you can e-mail him with your thoughts about this book at: awolinsk@concentric.net

Now let's move onto the final page we will work on together.

The Last Page

et's move on to the third and last page that we will explore together. In this page, you will learn the HTML coding that creates an unordered list, and an ordered list. I have named this file **experiment.html**. Here is the HTML coding used to create the page, followed by a picture of the finished page:

```
<HTML>
<HEAD>
<TITLE>Finger to Floor Experiment
</TITLE>
</HEAD>
<BODY>
<HR>
<CENTER>
<H1>Fingertips Experiment</H1>
<HR>
</CENTER>
<P>
<B>Materials:</B>
<UL>
<LI>Meter stick to measure distance
from floor to fingertips
<LI>Height chart or tool to measure
a person's height
<LI>Pencil or pen
```

The Last Page

Fingertips Experiment

Materials:

- Meter stick to measure distance from floor to fingertips
- Height chart or tool to measure a person's height
- Pencil or pen
- Paper

Procedure:

1. Record the person's age.
2. Record the person's sex.
3. Measure and record the person's height.
4. Measure and record the distance from the floor to the person's fingertips.
5. Repeat the procedure with as many subjects as you can.
6. Compile the data and analyze it.
7. Write your conclusions.

[BACK]

Here is what you will see on the last page of our Web site.

```
<LI>Paper
</UL>
<B>Procedure:</B>
<OL>
<LI>Record the person's age.
<LI>Record the person's sex.
<LI>Measure and record the person's
height.
<LI>Measure and record the distance
from the floor to the person's fin-
gertips.
<LI>Repeat the procedure with as
many subjects as you can.
<LI>Compile the data and analyze
them.
```

```
<LI>Write your conclusions.
</OL>
<HR>
<CENTER>
<A HREF="contents.html">[BACK]</A>
</CENTER>
<HR>
</BODY>
</HTML>
```

When you look at the picture of the page, you will notice two lists. One list is indented and has round bullets in front of each list item, and the other has numbers. They are both created in the same way, and there is only one small difference in the tags.

Let us examine the bulleted list.

```
<UL>
<LI>Meter stick to measure distance
from floor to fingertips
<LI>Height chart or tool to measure
a person's height
<LI>Pencil or pen
<LI>Paper
</UL>
```

It is called an unordered list and starts with the <UL> tag. After the starting tag comes each list item. The list item starts with the <LI> tag. The <LI> tag is another tag that leaves it up to you whether to add the ending tag, </LI>. You could put in the </LI> at the end of each list item, however, it is not required, so I have not done so. You can have as many items in a list as you like.

The second list has numbers instead of bullets.

If you are not sure of some techniques or want to explore some of the many other techniques not covered in this book, these are some sites you can visit:

<http://www.mcli.dist.maricopa.edu/tut/>

<http://www.ncsa.uiuc.edu/General/Internet/WWW/
   HTMLPrimerAll.html>

<http://www.cc.ukans.edu/~acs/index.shtml>

The numbers are made by the HTML code to create an ordered list. The only difference between making an unordered list and an ordered list is the beginning and ending tags. The ordered list starts with <OL> and ends with </OL>, whereas the unordered list starts with <UL> and ends with </UL>. There is actually only one letter difference between the creation of an ordered list and an unordered list.

You can now experiment with what you have created; you can change text, and you can add text until you have a Web site that you are proud of.

Finding a Home for Your Web Site

When you finish your Web site, you will need a place to publish it on the Internet. There are a few options. I cannot give you the specifics of what software to use and how to post your pages because the method varies from place to place, depending on where you are posting your page.

To post your pages, however, you need to have a place (Web server) on the Internet to store them and a way to get them from your computer to the Web server. Many Internet service providers give you from two to ten or more megabytes of storage space on one of their Web servers, for you to create your own Web site.

Call Around:

If you're looking for a home for your Web page, it may be best to start by calling local Internet service providers to see if they can help you.

Some service providers also offer templates and tools to bring interaction such as guest books and counters to your site. Some of the smaller service providers do not advertise posting personal Web pages because it is almost always a free service, and they do not profit from it. It also takes up space on their computer and makes more work for them.

The best way to find out what the situation is with your service provider is to call its technical-support number and ask whether they allow you to create personal Web pages. If they provide Web services, they will be able to give you the information you need.

Even if your service provider does not allow you to post personal Web pages, you can still put your pages on the Internet. There are a number of places on the Internet that offer you "free" Web space.

Did you notice the word *free* is in quotation marks? There is old expression, "There is no such thing as a free lunch." If someone offers you free Web space, you can be sure you are paying for it in some way. It may not cost you money, but you will be giving them something in return.

Most often, you will be giving them valuable information in return for the Web space. When you register for the Web site, you must provide them with information, which they can sell to others. Your name and e-mail address alone are worth plenty to them. The more information you provide, the more valuable it is, and the more it is costing you in loss of privacy.

The other thing you are giving to them is the eyes of the people who visit your pages. Whenever anyone visits your Web site, they will probably see

Internet Addresses	Internet Facts	On Your Screen

Here are some places that offer "free" Web sites. You can find more by doing a search for "free Web sites," using any major search engine:

<http://www.geocities.yahoo.com/home/>

<http://www.angelfire.com/>

<http://www.tripod.com/>

<http://www.cybercity.com/>

more than what you have posted. Very often, the first thing they see is a banner advertisement that pops up as soon as the page is visited.

Once you find a home for your Web pages, you need a way to get them from your computer to their new home. Once again, there are different ways of doing this, depending on your service provider or Web hosting site. If you have a regular Internet service provider, you may use FTP software to send the files from your computer to theirs. You can even use your Web browser to send files. Once again, a call to the Internet service provider's technical-support line should give you the information you need.

If you have one of the free services, you may be able to use regular FTP software, but more often you will use some specially designed Web pages that they provide to help you manage your site. Just locate the instructions, follow them carefully, and you will soon have your pages on the Internet.

Be Safe:
Don't give out any personal information on the Internet.

▶ Additional Information

You have learned the basics of creating Web pages, but there is much more to learn. For example, there are more ways of creating Web pages, programs to manage your Web site, ways to advertise your site, ways to get it listed in search engines, ways to make frames, ways to create forms for data collection, and many other topics I cannot cover in this book. If you want to find out more about these topics, you can visit my personal Web site. There you will find dozens of links not included in this book, and more information about how to get the most out of the Internet. The URL is

http://www.concentric.net/~awolinsk

I hope you now have a basic under-standing of how to publish Web pages on the Internet—and have had some fun figuring it out. May all your future Web pages be fun, exciting, and interesting.

See You Later . . .
Wow, we learned a lot about creating Web pages. I can't wait to start working on my own page. Good luck with yours!

Glossary

extensions—The three-letter endings after the period in a computer file name.

HREF—Hyper Reference.

HTML—HyperText Markup Language. A system of tags that tell a computer how to format text.

hyperlinks—Words, icons, or other images on a computer screen that, when clicked on, jump to another place.

IMG SRC—Image source, or the name of a picture computer file.

navigation bar—A guide on a Web page that consists of links and allows the user to move around the site.

paragraph tags—Tags that will create blank lines when formatting computer text.

URL—Universal resource locator. It is the address for any given Web site.

Web site plan—An outline, narrative, storyboard, or some other form that shows how a Web site will look when completed.

Further Reading

Computers and Children. Charleston, S.C.: Computer Training Clinic, 1994.

Henderson, Harry. *The Internet*. San Diego, Calif.: Lucent Books, 1998.

Mitchell, Kim. *Kids on the Internet: A Beginners Guide*. Grand Rapids, Mich.: Instructional Fair, 1998.

Moran, Barbara, and Kathy Ivens. *Internet Directory for Kids & Parents*. Foster City, Calif.: IDG Books Worldwide, 1998.

Rosner, Marc Alan. *Science Fair Success Using the Internet*. Springfield, N.J.: Enslow Publishers, Inc., 1999.

Index